The Job Hunting HERO Method:

Meeting and beating the challenges in

Landing That Job!

By: George Valentine

The Job Hunting Hero Method:

www.jobhunterstoolkit.com

jobhunterstoolkit@gmail.com

Table of Contents:

Acknowledgements and Introduction

Chapter One:

    Lesson #1: The Basics….. Page 3

Chapter Two:

    Lesson 2: Proving you have the Heart and Energy…. Page 16

Chapter Three:

    Lesson 3: Proving you can do the Relearning and Owning the Job…. Page 30

Chapter Four:

    Lesson 4: Putting It All Together …. Page 38

Dedication:

In special thanks, this book is dedicated to my two greatest heroes.

The first is my Lord and Savior and the second is the gift he gave to my life, my wife Karen. Learning through Him led me to Romans 5:1-5 which states that suffering produces endurance; endurance creates character and character, hope. Words to remember in the job hunt, eh? Learning through her has led me to understand more about life and true beauty than I would have ever thought was there.

I also dedicate my work to the people who face challenges in their life and in their job hunt – but they keep on moving forward.

Introduction to the HERO Method:

One of the most frustrating times in life is when you know that you are the right person for a job and not finding an employer who will take the chance and hire you. I do not have to tell you that, you are already facing the financial and emotional pressures of job hunting.

Through my years of helping people *land that job*, I find that people looking for work are often not speaking the employers' language or seeing the world from that person's perspective.

To gain an edge in the hunt, the hunter needs to first find their hidden skills and talents then help the employer understand the links between what the hunter offers and what the employer needs in a new employee.

In this workbook, first we will help you take a good and original look at the experience that you have such as whenever you have "done right" by someone else in meeting your responsibilities. Not only will this reflect well on you, it also shows that you are able to meet the challenges you have faced and have "done right" there as well. We will talk further on the HERO aspects later in the book.

We move on to understanding the four main aspects of a potential employee hiring managers look for, seeing the hunt from the employer's point of view (POV).

In today's job hunt, you have to make the connections between what the employer wants and what you offer. So for these four lessons, I will ask you to take a big step and stop thinking like a job hunter and more like a job provider. Stop wondering if your handshake is good enough, your cookie cutter resume is on the right color paper or if you need to invest in a new pair of "interview shoes". The HERO method requires that you think like the employer first and also know what it is you really offer.

Every job has a HERO, in that every job involves four aspects - Heart, Energy, Relearning things and Owning the work you do. You have those aspects already inside of you, built by the things you have done and the challenges you have faced. Through these four lessons, you will learn how you fit in these four aspects:

Heart: How well will you work with the customers, co-workers and stakeholders of the employer? Do you have the heart to make your work there a positive experience for everyone involved?

Energy: Do you have the level of energy needed for this job? Can you give steady effort to do the job well? This does not refer at all to a disabling condition, just that the employer understands you have the enthusiasm and drive needed for the position you are applying for?

Relearning: Do you have the ability to learn the new job so that you can do the job at the efficiency and effectiveness needed at the job? Can you learn the job promptly?

Owning It: Do you take responsibility for your actions – do you learn from your mistakes, work as hard when in good spirits as well as days that you are not feeling well, see the job as an extension of yourself?

By the time you have completed the lessons, you will have rewritten your applications, resume, JIST cards and other tools you are using in the job hunt so you can use the HERO Method to your advantage.

Just remember, please, the words of Mark Twain,

   "The secret to getting ahead is getting started."

And a quote from my old college roommate Andy who said

"A diamond is only a piece of coal that did well under pressure."

Now get out a pen that works and several pages of lined paper. Let's Get To Work!

You and the community:

List below the things you have done outside of work and family – clubs, sports, volunteering

In the first column write a title for what I did. Let us give a name to the work you have done – from bottle washer to coordinating an event. List each job separately.

In the second column: Describe duties for that work. Describe them in detail so that someone unfamiliar with the work would understand what you did. Instead of "built a swing for a community park" list who worked with you, tools you used, skills needed to do the job right.

In the third column: What I gained from it (skills, experience). You have gone through an experience you did not HAVE to do (you could have stayed home and eaten bon-bons, but you did not) What did you get out of the work done? List the skills sharpened, understandings, teamwork…

In the fourth column: My responsibilities (duties, actions)   What were the duties and responsibilities you had while you were there? List them and please do not be humble on this exercise.

Work Experience:

Something I did where I was given responsibility and I "did right by someone else"

In the first column: Title given by others

In the second column: Describe What I did in an average day. Please write this in detail, from start to finish. In this exercise, folks often find that they do more or in more detail than they originally realized.

In the third column: Responsibilities. Like you did in the earlier review of your work in the community, what were the responsibilities you had in the job so that if you did not do them or did not do them well, there would be problems for your clients or co-workers.

In the fourth column: Other things I did (trained others, etc.) Did you work double shifts on short notice? Did you train others or help others you worked alongside in the performance of the job?

Education and Training:

Things that I have learned to be good (proficient) at, whether in school, at a job

or in meeting personal and family needs.

In the first column: Area of learning. Let's give the material you learned a name that others will be able to understand and appreciate.

In the second column: Benefits to me. What did you get out of the learning you did. Please do not sugar coat this with phrases like "it made me a more worthwhile human being". What was it that this information did to change you and make you more proficient or broader in your view of the world.

In the third column: What I did w/the learning. List what it was that you have done with this learning. Feel free to say "nothing much" for only a few items.

In the fourth column: How I know I am good at it. Good! You have learned something – but how do you know you have learned – did you get a certificate, were you able to do something you were unable to do before?

(Note that learning things such as emergency medical treatment for a family member or learning accounting for a community club are valuable and should be listed.)

Please continue adding things in this section and use extra paper as you may need them. This lesson forms the foundation for how you will meet the HERO needs of an employer.

Picturing four employers

The next step is to show how each employer and prospective job has unique qualities of their own. This section requires you to **take the point of view of different employers**.

Please consider four employers you can picture yourself working at because until you can picture yourself working there, the employer surely will not.

In each case, you need to consider the four keys of HERO, Heart, Energy, ReLearning and Owning the Job.

Take your time with this section because you probably are not in the habit of taking the perspective of the employer in your job hunt.

In answering the questions remember: "***you can't paint over rust.***"

By that I mean that if you try to paint over the "rust" or problems in your past with flowery language or something not quite true, they will eventually break through that thin paint of language and lies and show themselves as rust again. Just be truthful and … Let's get to it.

First Job: Name of employer

_____

Name of job title I am hunting

_____

Heart: The clients or consumers I will be dealing with in the job, what are they like?

_____
_____

What do they want me to do for them?

_____
_____

What is an example of a difficult situation I may be in with them/ how would I handle that?

Co-workers: What are they like?

_____
_____
_____
_____

Are we working together toward a goal or more individually?

_____
_____

What is an example of a difficult situation I may be in with them?

_____
_____

How well do I understand the co-workers and management points of view?

_____
_____

Stakeholders: People or organizations you do not usually interact with but they are affected by your work.

Who are they and how would I interact with them?

_____
_____

Second Job: Name of employer

_____

Name of job title I am hunting

_____

Heart: The clients or consumers I will be dealing with in the job, what are they like?

_____
_____

What do they want me to do for them?

_____
_____

What is an example of a difficult situation I may be in with them/ how would I handle that?

_____
_____
_____

Co-workers: What are they like?

_____
_____
_____

Are we working together toward a goal or more individually?

_____

_____

What is an example of a difficult situation I may be in with them?

_____

_____

How well do I understand the co-workers and management points of view?

_____

_____

Stakeholders

Who are they and how would I interact with them?

_____

_____

Third Job: Name of employer

_____

Name of job title I am hunting

_____

Heart: The clients or consumers I will be dealing with in the job, what are they like?

_____
_____

What do they want me to do for them?

_____
_____

What is an example of a difficult situation I may be in with them/ how would I handle that?

_____
_____
_____

Co-workers: What are they like?

_____

_____

_____

Are we working together toward a goal or more individually?

_____

_____

What is an example of a difficult situation I may be in with them?

_____

_____

How well do I understand the co-workers and management points of view?

_____

_____

Stakeholders

Who are they and how would I interact with them?

_____

_____

Fourth Job: Name of employer

_____

Name of job title I am hunting

_____

Heart: The clients or consumers I will be dealing with in the job, what are they like?

_____
_____

What do they want me to do for them?

_____
_____

What is an example of a difficult situation I may be in with them/ how would I handle that?

_____
_____
_____

Co-workers: What are they like?

_____
_____
_____

Are we working together toward a goal or more individually?

_____

_____

What is an example of a difficult situation I may be in with them?

_____

_____

How well do I understand the co-workers and management points of view?

_____

_____

Stakeholders

Who are they and how would I interact with them?

_____

_____

You do not need to have *specifically* the same experiences in the new job as you have had in the past, you only need to be able to appreciate the viewpoints, needs and concerns of the people you would be dealing with in the new job.

Heart:

My clients, customers or patients have expectations of the quality of service they can expect. What have you done in the past to meet the expectations of people you have served?

_____
_____
_____
_____
_____

My agency needs to find ways of attracting and maintaining clients. What have you done, what can you do to help in these ways?

_____
_____
_____
_____

Often it is important to see the world from the client's point of view to better serve them. Give two examples of how you can see the world from another's needs and point of view.

_____
_____
_____
_____

Joining our team will take some adjustments on your part. What are examples of your working well alongside others?

_____
_____
_____
_____
_____

_____

We have many stakeholders – people who have a stake in the performance of our agency. What are examples of how you have worked well with people in a different position from you who have a stake in an outcome you agree to.

_____
_____
_____
_____
_____

_____

Below write of how you have shown you have the heart – compassion, empathy, caring for another that makes you special and unique – related or unrelated to the job you are applying for.

Energy: What level of energy is required for the job?

On a 'good day' at work what are the physical and emotional challenges I will face?

_____
_____

_____
_____

On a 'bad day' at work, what are the physical and emotional challenges I will face?

_____
_____
_____
_____

Re-learning: Ability to learn what is needed for the job efficiently and effectively.

What kind of things will I have to learn or adapt to in order to do the job well?

_____
_____
_____
___

Is there a lot of training as systems keep changing?

_____
_____
_____

How will I know I have learned the job well?

_____
_____

Owning the Job: Being honest and true to the quality of work you do.

The employer needs to know that people will be responsible for the work they do, good and bad. I need to know you will support and defend my company and its consumers the best you can.

If someone does not accept correction and criticism here, can you?

_____

_____

We need to care for the quality of work that leaves this place, what is your experience in keeping an eye to detail?

_____

_____

_____

My name is on the door and on every letter that goes out, what is your level of responsibility and can you handle it?

_____

_____

_____

You need to defend our reputation to our clients; can you handle the requirements of confidentiality, consistent customer service, etc.? Give an example of a situation where you would do this.

_____

_____

_____

Now onto the work of putting what you know into something that can help move you to a brighter future.

Lesson II: Heart and Energy

"I don't know about the secret to success, but the secret to failure is trying to please everybody."

Bill Cosby, comedian, philosopher

Heart: In the first part of the HERO method we look at what you offer when it comes to "heart" issues. Employers want to know that you have the heart for the job in that you will:

- get along and work well with the consumers or clients of what you will be doing;

- co-workers at all levels of the job

- the other 'stakeholders' of the agency.

By stakeholders, I mean the people who have a stake in what the company or agency does – the public, the company shareholders, the media and other people you will occasionally come in contact with in the course of the job.

Each job has a different range of clients, coworkers and stakeholders, such as at the department store floor where you are working with other clerks, customers, the human resources department… a large number of people and different types of interactions every day. The employer will size you up and see if she thinks you have what it takes so you either will get along well or at least not cause new problems.

How will you show that? By understanding and expressing in the employer's language the "heart" track record you have to run on.

Take a look at the lists you have made in the first lesson, especially the one where you made a detailed list of the different things you have done in life either in work, volunteer or life experience. Now break that down based on the way you interacted with other people in the following tables.

By that I mean the type of interactions you had, the kind of people you worked with and the objectives of that work. Take your time with this one because it is the first practice and you may need to return to it again and again as you get a better understanding of the power of the HERO method.

OK, go to it...

HEART: Work and life experience.

In the first column: Where I was: Describing the specific place you worked at and the interactions you had with others.

In the second column: People I worked with or helped. Describing them and the challenges that thy faced. Also describe how you have changed through learning to see the world through another person's perspective.

In the third column: Objective of that work: What did you – or the other person – want to accomplish through your interaction. How well were you able to accomplish those goals through your point of view – and theirs.

The next stage is for you to see the jobs you have selected for your hunt and see the role of "heart" from the employer's point of view (POV). This may take research on your part by asking others familiar with the company or the services they offer what they may see as the people and stakeholders involved in the job.

This research is well worth it and the benefits back to you will set you apart from others vying for the same job. Because this will promote a change in the way you see the world, take a few minutes and try by yourself or get others involved in this exercise, too.

HEART: Employer's POV *People you serve:*

Who they are (characteristics)
:_____
_____
_____
_____

What are they expecting from you (their objectives):_____
_____
_____
_____

Can you see the world from their POV?
_____

_____
_____
_____

Is there stress/tension in your relationship with them?
(Describe):_____
_____
_____
_____
_____
_____

Co Workers:

Who they are (experience, education, and job description):_____
_____

_____
_____
_____

What are they expecting from you (getting along, independent thought,
etc.)_____
_____
_____

Is there stress/tension expected in your relationship (how to handle that):_____

_____

Stakeholders:

Who are they? (Describe):_____

_____
_____
_____

What do they expect from you?

_____
_____
_____

Can you see the world from their Point of View?

_____
_____
_____

General Issues: **For each of the groups, review these three questions.**

Customers:

What kinds of problems or conflicts can you expect to have on the job?

_____
_____
_____

Have you dealt with these kinds of conflicts or problems before and how well did you do with them?

_____
_____
_____
_____

Co Workers:

What kinds of problems or conflicts can you expect to have on the job?

_____
_____
_____

Have you dealt with these kinds of conflicts or problems before and how well did you do with them?

_____
_____
_____
_____

Stakeholders:

What kinds of problems or conflicts can you expect to have on the job?

_____
_____
_____

Have you dealt with these kinds of conflicts or problems before and how well did you do with them?

_____
_____
_____
_____

Did you notice the slight twists toward the end there? Being able to see the world from another's point of view is essential in today's job market. This is what separates you from the next applicant who is only looking for some job and is not putting in the "heart" to understand the world around them.

By showing not only that you take the effort to see the world from different POV's, you also indicate that you have specific examples of how you have 'walked the walk' and have done this in the past. You are getting ready to become that HERO.

Take a moment and think through the different jobs where **heart** is essential to the job –

- **Health care**: Whether you work with the elderly, in a hospital or in a medical office, your ability to understand *how the client sees the world* and your role *in their world* makes you a better applicant and later a more valued employee. Think of the differences you have found in employees you have met through your role as the patient or the family member of a patient when you found an employee with a real "heart" for the job.

- **Customer Service**: The next time you go shopping, notice the number of clerks who genuinely make eye contact with you. Something so small as a glance means a lot to the customer's experience. Getting along with management and co-workers is often a make-or-break issue for the people who will stay on and the people who do not last in the retail business.

- **Communications**: Although this is often seen as a job that is all about speaking or writing skill, it also requires the heart to work well with others and appreciating the people around you. In journalism or public relations for a company, it is important to get along well with co-workers.

Now we review the exercises for this lesson so far. Take a look at what the "heart" demands of the job will be for the positions you are hunting and compare that with the experiences you already have had.

Try matching them up and making indirect connections where direct ones may not seem to exist. THIS is where you will make the case that YOU are the person for the job. For example:

- **Health care**: Let's say you cared for your grandmother, helping her make it to medical appointments and being there with her when she had sudden trips to the hospital. Maybe you worked with disabled kids at a summer youth camp and won a camp award for your work with them. These experiences show that you have an understanding of the world from the POV of people who are different from yourself and in need of special care and attention. It also shows that you have dealt with coworkers, nurses and doctors.

- **Customer Service:** If you worked afterschool in a grocery store, mostly stocking shelves with other staff. This job required sometimes helping direct customers to what they wanted, bagging groceries and bringing them out to customer's cars. Think through all the things you did in that work and you should find some connection with serving the public.

- **Communications**: Let's say you worked on your high school radio station or newspaper and helped with getting the word out about a local festival. This along with any education in the fields shows that you have an understanding about the roles different people play in communications and that you will get the job done working with them.

What can I do to improve my "heart?"

The answer here depends partly on the type of work you are pursuing as 'heart' will mean different things to different employers.

For example, employers with jobs which require more attention to serving others may want to see your ability to work with people different from yourself. For this, showing how you have dealt with a range of people will help – for example through your place of worship, school, helping customers, etc. You can improve this by focusing on your communications skills and moving toward opportunities where you interact with clients or customers.

Other employers would want to focus on co-workers and your ability to work with a group of people toward accomplishing a goal. Consider your personal history where this may have happened and on situations where you may be able to work with others as peers. For example, working to put on a festival or fundraiser is a great role for showing your co-worker skills.

Finally, other employers may be concerned that you can deal with people who may have other agendas or who are on a different level from your role. People who write press releases, parents who work with committees on the handicapped or who have extensive dealings with doctors to help a loved one may be examples here.

__Below write examples of how you may be able to improve your "heart" aspect in the employer's perspective.__

Energy:

One of the spoken (or sometimes unspoken) questions the employer has in an interview is "why is working for me important to you?"

The underlying POV here is a concern that you will not have the enthusiasm or level of energy they want from a great or even a good employee. If working for me is important to you, it will show in the energy you bring to the job and to the interactions you will have with my consumers.

One of the greatest phrases I have learned in the job hunting field is

"you can't teach drive".

By that I mean that drive and enthusiasm is not something in a bottle or in a textbook and you either bring it to the job or you do not. The employer wants to know that you will have the energy level needed and that you can "turn it on" when the job responsibilities call for it.

How can I prove to the employer I have the energy needed/wanted in an employee?

Other job hunters have all read the same books and they can show in an interview the enthusiastic handshake, sitting leaning forward during the interview and on and on.

You should have examples of how you have been able to provide the same amount of drive on good days as well as bad ones. Examples separate you from people who just show enthusiasm in an interview.

How do I stand out? With the facts such as examples of how you have faced the crises for your family members or in your own life; how you have been part of clubs, teams or community organizations; how you have joined with others to help solve problems.

The work you have done for your friends, family and community can stand out. So let us return to your Lesson I and look at it from the POV of how you have shown you have energy and spirit.

ENERGY:

Remember that most of the good in the world is done by people who are too tired, old, fat, sleepy, disabled, discouraged (or fill in the blank with another excuse) to do it, but they did it anyway.

THAT ...

is the enthusiasm and dedication employers are looking for in a great employee. Show it in your stride and handshake, sure. But through the HERO method, you will have some specific proof that is more than just talk.

Now the employer has certain ways of looking at drive as well. As with HEART, the opportunity here is to understand the employer's perspective and tie your experiences to what they are looking for.

In the first column: Where I was/ my role it in: By this I mean what was your role in relationship to both your co-workers and the people your company served.

In the second column: Examples of energy needed. In the work you were responsible for, what was the energy level required and what were the kinds of work – physical labor and brain work – needed to do the job consistently well?

In the third column: Objective of the work/outcomes: Really give this one some thought. Instead of saying :stacking pallets" make sure to note that you had to do them quickly in coordination with other workers and effectively so that they would not come crashing down in the middle of your shift.

Energy: Employer's POV:

I want someone who faces problems head-on. Give examples of how/when you worked to resolve a tough problem:

_____
_____
_____
_____

_____
_____

And another problem:

_____
_____
_____
_____
_____

And another problem:

_____
_____
_____
_____

_____
_____

I want someone who has worked hard when it was not expected, like overtime, or on a team practicing in the rain, something like that. Any examples?

_____
_____
_____
_____
_____
_____

And another example?

_____
_____
_____

–

Everyone "hits the wall" and cannot work any further. Give an example of what it takes to exhaust you (this shows you understand your limitations):

_____
_____
_____

_____
_____
_____

I like people who volunteer or do more than what is expected, when they do not have to. Any examples?

_____
_____
_____
—

Another example?

_____
_____
_____
—

Now is the opportunity to connect what you have done in work or in life experience to the needs of the employer. This area gives you the opportunity to speak a bit more personally and to connect with the employer on more than a "hire me please" level, so have some fun with it.

Some examples of areas where the energy issue is especially important include:

- **<u>Office Clerking</u>**: Maybe you helped in organizing the estate information after an uncle passed away and that took a lot of work **and attention to detail**. (this is another example of energy) Experience as the treasurer of a high school club or a role with a labor union which had unexpected work regularly (this also shows respect of my peers in a position like that) both show energy.

- **Human Services**: I helped in a child care center, often working late when the parents did not arrive on time and resolving problems, addressing emergencies as they came up.

- **Warehousing**: For three years I worked regularly lifting items and working alongside other staff, including **training others** in the work to be done. (Note that they would not have *just anyone* training new staff, the employer saw something in the quality of your work, so make sure to mention when you trained others.)

Please make sure to return to review and add to the first and second lessons in the future adding to your lists as you recall things you have done from the HERO perspective.

What can I do to improve my "energy"?

This is a tough one because so many people are well versed in how to show enthusiasm and energy to a prospective employer. The good news is that unless they can back it up with an example or two, they blend in with all of the other people who "talk the talk" but may not show that they have ever "walked the walk".

As you list what you can do, think of the times you went above and beyond the job or volunteer description *and please do not be humble on this one*. Review the list of the times you worked overtime on short notice; training you took or when you trained others or sports you played in which show you know "how to break a sweat".

Looking forward, **get involved in something where you did more than what is expected** in your role as a parent or sibling, citizen or member of an organization. What is it about your life and responsibilities generally - such as being a naturally busy person and keeping it all together - that is important information to the employer as well.

One thing to remember as you move forward in job hunting. It is important to show the same energy to the first prospective employer you meet on a sunny day as you do with the fifth on a rainy, cold day. The best way I can relate this to you is something basketball coaches like me say before a tough game.

You tell your team that maybe that other team would beat you nine times out of any ten times you play them. Well, what if today is that **one** in ten chance?

You may need to knock on ten doors this week to get one good lead – who is to say the next one is that one? Prepare and try like THIS is your one in ten time.

Congratulations on your work thus far. On to Lesson III and Relearning and Owning It.

Lesson III:

Relearning and Owning It

In this lesson we review two more essential keys for any new job. Do you have the aptitude to learn a new skill (re-learning parts in a new way) and the courage and conscientiousness to work hard and have a sense of owning the work you do?

The important point about re-learning is that there are very few job-employee combinations where the individual already knows all there is to learn about the new position. As technology changes and job descriptions and responsibilities remain in flux, every new hire needs to learn what the job will require today and in the future.

Relearning:

As noted in the introduction to the book, re-learning means the ability to learn the job efficiently so that the new hire will be able to do it effectively and reliably do the job in a relatively short amount of time. It also includes the ability to adapt to changes in the way things are done without a large investment of time and resources by the employer.

Before we review your answers from the first lesson, two short games:

- **Teaching aliens about baseball (or music or makeup)**

Pretend that a friendly visitor from another planet has arrived on earth and by the miracles of your imagination can speak your language. This alien turns to you and asks "what is this game 'baseball' I hear about, can you tell me fifteen things about it? (You can substitute the alien asking about a musical instrument or make-up instead). Go ahead and make that list of things you know about baseball – the equipment, famous players, the rules, etc.

"Now, please ten more to your list," he says.

The alien is impressed and states *you must do this for a living since you know it so well.*

The moral of this exercise is that here is something you have learned about and know pretty well **and it does not help you pay your rent**. Think of how much more you have the capacity and interest in learning was topic or skill that WILL help you pay the rent. Do not consider you are unable to learn a new field… you've already shown you can teach an alien about baseball.

Also note that there was a time when you did not know how to button a shirt or tie your shoes, but now you could probably do them in the dark – you have learned because it benefitted you to learn.

- **The Janitor Game:**

Select a job you have done, either for pay or as a volunteer. Now list all the aspects of the position from when you started to when you ended. Now list all you would do in the job from the start to the end of the day and keep these lists to yourself.

Now, tell a friend **just the title of the job** only and ask them to describe ten or fifteen responsibilities or actions the average person would do in that job. With luck, you will be surprised to see how your list includes things he or she would not have even thought of.

It's called the janitor game because people are often limited in their understanding of what a job title really includes. As a janitor, maybe the person worked alone and was given the keys to work in an empty office; maybe they had to learn about chemicals and how they react in different situations; maybe worked in an office area or a gymnasium or maybe they had to train others or to work longer shifts unexpectedly.

Hidden behind the job title are many aspects the employer may find as important to the hiring decision. That janitor's ability to work independently or willingness to work longer hours or ability to learn quickly how chemicals effect what is cleaned may help the employer see that he is the right person for the job.

The moral of the exercise is never sell yourself and your work short because a title does not reflect all you did. Remember that some aspects of the job that people may not know you did can show your connection to the needs of the new job.

Now back to relearning by reviewing what it is you have done in the past. Get out your lists from Lesson I and list them below:

Re-learning:

In the first column: Position title. This is more for keeping track of the work you have done.

In the second column: What I had to know to do the job. What did you have to know to do the job efficiently and effectively over time. What did you have to do in order to be adaptable to the changes that occurred in the job.

In the third column: How quickly did I learn/adapt

What can I do to improve my "re-learning"

The best way to picture this is facet is remembering that one candle illuminates a dark room. Studying a field generally gives you an understanding of what it is about and indicates your interest/possible aptitude in that field. If you want to consider bookkeeping, then take a course, such as the ones available **free** online through Massive Open enrollment Online Courses, MOOC.

MOOC is the abbreviation for a whole world of free courses you can take from your computer. and are available in almost every field from colleges and universities around the world. Do a search for "MOOC list" and see what I mean.

You can also gain some knowledge in a field by volunteering or interning in a local not-for-profit agency locally. Many agencies would welcome the opportunity to have an enthusiastic new helper either as a volunteer or an intern offering a general or more specific investment of time.

One-stop employment centers across the United States (go to www.servicelocator.org for more information) may provide training or can refer you to places that can help you get the help you need such as wage subsidy programs or on-the-job training placements.

Owning It:

This key refers to taking responsibility for your hard work by being conscientious, gaining through constructive criticism or correction from others and from being honest. This often is the hardest part of HERO to put into action in an interview with the employer but also one of the most important.

First, let us go over your work and personal history as it relates to Owning It. First go over the times you met stressful situations and came out stronger. Notice that you did not have to have the experience on the job – it could be a mistake you made in a sport; through a situation at school or home. Just give a sample of how you are a responsible person and have a talent and maturity the employer would want on his team.

In the first column: Describe experience. Describe it in detail so that someone unfamiliar with the experience would understand it and your role in it.

In the second column: What made it hard/stressful. Feel free to be detailed in this. Remember that in a situation you may have gotten used to over time, there was still stress involved.

In the third column: Specifics of experience/what's learned. How were you changed through the experience – what did you learn from the beginning to the end?

Now the employer's POV in Owning It:

I want an employee who I can give a job and walk away knowing it will be done right. Do you have that kind of independent experience?

_____
_____
_____
_____

I want to be able to call you on and have you correct your mistakes and know I am not just 'talking to the air'. Will you listen and change? Give me an example.

I want to know you have taken personal responsibility when a problem has arisen and you did your best to correct it. Give me an example of accepting you made a mistake and correcting it.

_____
_____
_____
_____

Will you take responsibility for the decisions you have made or will you try to hand off to others what you have done?

_____

_____

_____

What can I do to improve my "owning it"

In its most direct form, 'owning it' is the ability to accept challenges, mistakes and problems and to act on them with honesty and maturity. Employers want to know that the people they hire have integrity and have experience meeting problems with the interest and the ability to solve them.

As with energy, people can talk a good game but the bonus goes to people who can show they have demonstrated this quality. Look back on your scholastic, personal and work life and think of the challenges you faced and the decisions you have made when the pressure was on.

One question employers often ask is to tell them of a weakness you have. HERE is the opportunity to say how you recognize a personal flaw and the efforts you have made to address or correct the flaw.

Moving forward, take a look at what has held you back - problems in taking orders, managing time, etc. and give examples of how that has hurt in the past, take responsibility for that and now show how you have grown from it.

One way to improve your owning it factor is to identify a personal weakness or poor decision made and actively find a way to address this flaw - first by making lists of the flaws and the resources you have around you to practice getting better and addressing what may be holding you back.

By taking what Alcoholics Anonymous calls **a moral inventory** (asking friends for help on this one), you can address what is wrong and show you can "own" yourself.

Maybe you face special challenges in life. This may lead to your being able to offer the employer the Worker Opportunity Tax Credit for hiring you instead of the next applicant.

"Target populations" of people who have faced special challenges to landing a job (veterans, single parents, folks with a disabling condition, etc.) may qualify for giving their employer a tax credit worth hundreds or thousands of dollars for hiring them instead of the next person. Check out the "WOTC" to see if you may qualify, make your first impression, and then tell the employer of their great fortune if they are smart enough to hire you.

As you keep moving forward toward your dreams remember what I teach each the job hunters I work with:

Every great idea, every great dream begins with one person thinking it's a good idea and a thousand people saying to him or her 'what? Are you crazy?' Just know that this is expected – go follow those dreams even with a plurality of one.

Lesson IV:
Putting It To Work

First of all, congratulations on making it to Lesson IV of the HERO method. You are seeing the world a little differently now and view your own skills and talents a little differently as well. Now we finally get to put it into practice to build new and better job hunting tools for the hunt.

In each step, please remember that the goal is to better understand the POV of the person making the hiring decision because in the end, it is that point of view that makes the difference.

* **Your resume**: Take each of the four prospective employers you listed in Lesson I and consider how best to put your experience into their language. Review step by step the answers you have made about the employer's POV and list your experiences with those concerns in mind.

Often people will use bullets (short sentences or phrases which describe the work done) to spotlight and help direct the employer to different things the hunter wants them to see.

Note – this probably requires you write resumes customized to each of the different employers.

For example, if you want to show that you have the heart for working with disabled persons, you may use your phrases to show you have worked helping people with limitations, have experience in human services or have sensitivity to people different from yourself.

Indicate in your work or personal experience sections of your resume that you have that in your background.

Practice by first writing a long list of the bullets you feel are related to what the employer is looking for then later pare down the list to the ones you feel best state what you want to say. Do this bullet writing and paring so that each of the four sections of the HERO method are used.

In the end, the resume should cover the range of what you have done either in a functional or chronological resume – it is YOUR story after all – but make certain to include the bullets most essential to what the employer is looking for.

When you have completed your draft resume, have it reviewed by someone else. That someone should be a person you trust and someone you can take constructive criticism from.

* **Your job application**: This is the listing of your contact information, references, and hours of availability. It is the standardized first assignment for the person who will ultimately land the job. Take it as a work assignment and be clear, concise and NEAT about it.

Be clear and concise because (please remember this) "whenever an employer's mind drifts (from vague answers) it *always* drifts away from you." Bullets about responsibilities connected to the work of the new job are your best chance for getting called in for an interview.

All you want from the application is to still be in the running after it has been reviewed.

For example, under 'hours available' do NOT list, say 9 AM to 5 PM if you are actually available for hours earlier in the day and later in the day. You do not yet know when the first shift of the day begins – so for right now in the application – make yourself as available as possible.

That is all you are hoping from in an application - not to be overlooked and to get that interview.

For 'job responsibilities and related sections, use the bullets written in Lessons II and III to say what you have done and can do. Please write your hours of availability and bullets below.

* **Your JIST cards**: JIST cards are index style cards that you can give to the prospective employer highlighting the parts of your experience that make you a strong candidate for the job.

These are not "thank you for meeting with me" cards or something you give little thought to. After you have gained a greater sense of what the job entails, have already sent in a resume or met with the employer, a JIST card may be just the difference in landing the job or not.

At this point in the hunt, the employer has your application and knows your resume but a little boost may set you apart from the crowd.

These cards can be written to show in bulleted form how you have the heart, energy, relearning ability and ownership of the job to be a great new hire. You would send it along either with a cover letter or dropped off with the employer's hiring manager, complete with your contact information. It is a time proven way to keep your name and skills before the employer.

List below what you would put in a JIST card for each of the four employers you are targeting.

Your interview preparation: Remember that the employer has three basic questions in mind – tell me about yourself (what about you is connected to being a good member of my team?); why do you want to work for me? (show that you will put in extra effort for working here) and why should I pick you over the next person who comes in my door?

The HERO method helps you address each of the three main questions of the interview:

- Telling about yourself – select the bullets that connect most closely to the strengths you have in your application. If you most closely meet the employer's POV in learning, lead with that, but make certain to cover the bottom line question of what makes you a good pick for this job.

- Why work for me? Here you show that you have the energy and dedication to do THIS job and that through your other experiences you can show that this line of work and or this specific employer are right for you.

- Why hire you and not someone else? You now have written in detail why YOU are the best candidate. During the course of the interview have a few examples in mind and mention a few of them when the time is right.

Write below your answers to these basic questions and practice saying your answers aloud.

As you prepare for the next step, be careful that your words are clear and do not just lead to more questions. As the philosopher Rodney Dangerfield said:

> **"I went to my doctor and he told me 'You're crazy!"**
>
> **I said, "Doc, I think I want a second opinion" so the doctor said**
>
> **"and you're ugly, too."**

By practicing your answers and making sure they stand alone and need not lead to either new questions or the employer's mind wandering, you get to showcase why hiring you is such a great idea. Now before we go…

Some parting thoughts:

In order to meet and defeat the challenges you are facing, **you need to practice** what you have learned before you go out to meet the employers. First of all, *practice* what you are going to say.

> *Do not take my word for it;*
>
> *consider the story of Stan and Bruno, the talking dog:*

Stan, down on his luck and with little money, sat quietly with his dog Bruno in a park at favorite bench near the river. Stan sighed and idly asked his dog what he wanted to do. To his surprise the dog said "I bet you'd like to take a swim. Hhey, I'd like to join you."

Stan just stared as the silence between them grew. The dog spoke again "Hey, those Yankees are doing pretty well, huh? Girardi's a great coach."

"Bruno! You can talk! We're going to be rich!! A talking dog, yahoo! We're going to that talent agent downtown right now!"

Bruno said, **"Hey, Stan, we should practice what we are going to say!"** Stan said "no time to waste, we'll just start talking – it will be great!"

They reached the office building with a huge sign reading "Cash in on your talent" on top, then walked down the long hallway of photos of stars and on into her office.

The talent agent said "this better be good, most animal acts are not worth my time. "

Stan: "No problem. Hey Bruno, what is on top of this building?"

Bruno: "Roof! Roof!" **The agent just stared.**

Stan: "Let's try this one – Bruno, tell her about the hard times we have had, me without a job…"

Bruno: "Rough, rough". The agent said "One last chance or I throw you out."

Stan: "OK, OK, Bruno… you're a big baseball fan, you love the Yankees, right? Who is the greatest Yankee ballplayer of all time?"

Bruno smiled and proudly said "Ruth, Ruth!"

The agent kicked them out of her office. Stan and Bruno sadly walked back to their bench. Bruno looked sadly at Stan and said "**We really should have practiced**. And I probably should have said Joe DiMaggio."

Folks, **don't be like Stan** – listen to your inner Bruno and practice aloud the answers you may bring to an interview.

Remember the Lumberjack:

When trying to chop a log with an axe, sometimes people only chip off a small piece of wood. After trying and trying, they may not have much to show for their efforts for a while because looking at it from the outside not much seems to be happening. Do not despair, hunter.

On the inside of the log, things are changing, bonds are breaking making it easier with each new swing to eventually meet the goal and split the log.

Job hunting is often like this in that you try hard with each swing – each new contact and job listing and resume and interview. When not much seems to be happening remember, that is only what is happening on the outside. On the inside you are learning about what works, what feels real to you. Little by little more people are learning that there is a dynamic and capable person looking for work. With each swing, you are getting closer to your goal, just have faith that it will all turn out alright.

> **Make a list of the swings or efforts you take each week in your job hunt.**
>
> **As you prepare for the future, make a list of what actions you guarantee you will make each day or week no matter the weather or distractions or discouragements that come your way because, hey, you never know what the next 'swing' will bring:**

Partner Up:

There is an old Texas expression **that any mule can knock a building down, but it takes a good man or woman to build one up.**

Now that you have gone through these lessons, help other people to build that special future for themselves. In helping others you are able to better understand and put into practice what you know in job hunting for yourself and you will also get that priceless feeling that someone else's life is better because of your words and actions.

Also, make sure to thank the people who help you along the way. They have been seeing something in you maybe even before you saw it in yourself. Honor that with a thank you. They were your hero all along.

Congratulations on completing this book and good luck in the future.

www.ingramcontent.com/pod-product-compliance
Lightning Source LLC
Chambersburg PA
CBHW071759170526
45167CB00003B/1088